A BASQUE DIARY

LIVING IN HONDARRIBIA

BY ALEX HALLATT

For our teachers and friends in the Basque Country:
Gloria, Bernard, Andoni, Carmen, Rafa, Itziar, Edu, Idoia, Marina, Borja (2), Gorka (2), Evelyn, Patrick, Natalia, Julena, Aitziber, Arantza, Tamara, Iker, Laida, Vanessa, Miren, Gorka, Maria, Olga, Biru, Zuri, Agustina, Javier, Len, Mari Carmen, Maribel, Rosa, Silvia, Yulia, Maruchi, Mayi, Almudena, Iñaki (2), Clementina, Mari Carmen, Carlos, Sean, Elena, Adriana, Terra, Billy, Renata, Cris, Pia, Juanita, and all the other people in Hondarribia who we knew more by sight than by name.

And thank you to Duncan, who has shared these adventures and has encouraged and helped in their publication.

CONTENTS

INTRODUCTION

Lots of Brits go to Spain for the better weather. No one goes to the Basque Country for the weather. It is a land of pointy green hills, dotted with caseríos (traditional Basque smallholdings) and beautiful valleys pocked with ugly factories. The coast is ruggedly gorgeous, with forests and sheep pasture falling into sloping layers of schist rock. But, as in the UK, the lush beauty of the countryside comes from the fact that it rains a lot at any time of year, though especially in the winter.

In our first months of being here, we asked locals what the winters were like. They mimed hara-kiri. They warned us that, in the dark days of winter, people get depressed due to the wind, rain and cold. I hate wind, rain and cold, but I needn't have worried, because there is

From Hendaye, you can see the ugly tower blocks that flank Hondarribia beach. But you can also see the caserios in the lovely hills behind it.

no way that the weather is as bad as it is in England. In the two years we lived in the Basque Country we enjoyed great weather, often ten degrees or so warmer than the UK. It's not always sunny and warm, but sometimes you have to get things done (I had my cartooning deadlines to meet and Duncan was keen to study his Spanish) and that's a lot easier when it isn't glorious outside. And when a place doesn't have the best weather, it usually develops and maintains an interesting culture. That is true for England and doubly so for the Basque Country.

The reason we went to the Basque Country was to learn Spanish. It is a bi-lingual region. Many people speak Basque as their first language, but others living there don't speak much Basque at all. Sometimes this is because of the legacy of Franco (who banned the teaching and speaking of Basque). Other times it is because of people moving into the area from other parts of Spain. The upshot is that nearly everyone speaks Spanish. Unlike in the Spanish towns more popular with English tourists, very few people speak more than a few words of English. They are more likely to speak French because of being on the border with France. This made it the perfect place for us to practise our Spanish with native speakers.

Learning the language was one of the reasons we moved to the Basque Country. Our reasons for picking the small town (population: about 17,000) of Hondarribia were different. My first Spanish teacher had been from Donostia-San Sebastian and had waxed lyrical about this city (European City of Culture in 2016). I visited in December of 2007 and was blown away by the food, beaches and how pretty the city was. We came back to visit in the spring of 2013 and loved it. But it was busy (it gets crazy busy in summer) and Duncan wanted to live somewhere smaller. He had read a *New York Times* article (http://nyti.ms/1DvG2SF) about how Hondarribia is one of the best places to enjoy the region's cuisine and it was easy to get a bus there from Donostia, so we did.

We spent the day eating pintxos/pinchos (the Basque tapas) and drinking very affordable wine in Calle San Pedro in the Marina area (called this because this is reclaimed land and where the fishing boats used to come in.). We walked along the River Bidasoa to the beach, which at Easter was nearly empty (unlike La Concha in Donostia). We passed through the impressive medieval wall that surrounds the streets of the old town and admired the natural surroundings. Hondarribia is flanked on the west by the Jaizkibel range of hills, to the south by allotment gardens and wetlands, to the east by the River Bidasoa and to the north by the bay of Txingudi. Across the river is France and the surf beach at Hendaye. It seemed that Hondarribia had everything that we wanted (wild swimming, surfing and hill walking for me; great food and wine for Duncan).

Though there wasn't a lot of rental accommodation in the town (we made the mistake of moving to Hondarribia in the summer, when everyone wants to be there to escape the heat of the interior), what we found was cheaper than in Donostia. The food and drink is also about ten percent cheaper than Donostia. Being a smaller town, it seemed a lot easier to get to know people and to talk with them. We've made a lot of friends here.

The rhubarb is growing well in the community garden patch. Unlike the rosemary, it hasn't been dug up and stolen. Probably because rhubarb isn't as popular here as in England, or Australia* and New Zealand.

*where my rhubarb plant was stolen.

Hallatt

GEOGRAPHY AND GETTING AROUND

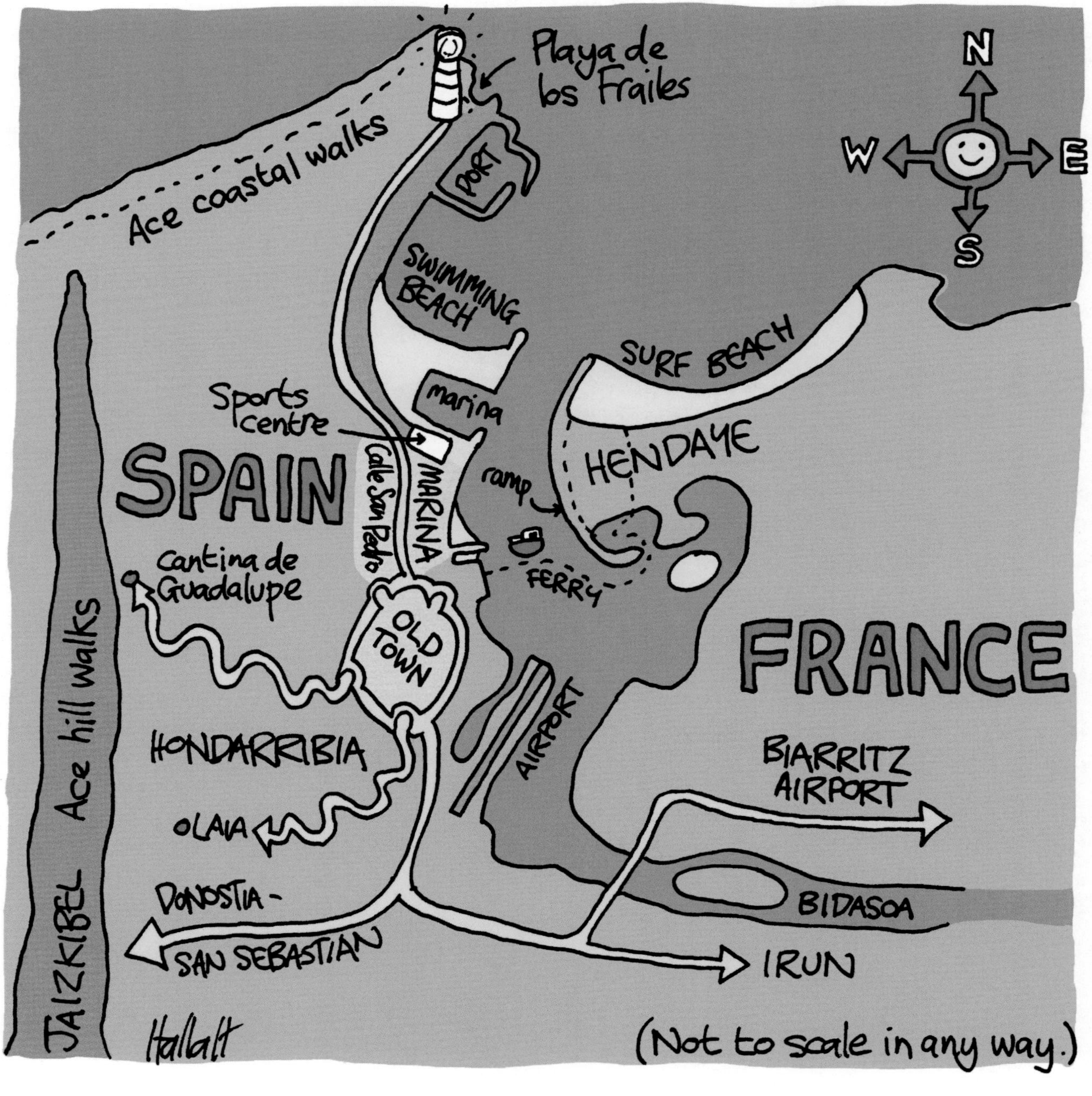
Playa de los Frailes
Ace coastal walks
PORT
SWIMMING BEACH
SURF BEACH
marina
Sports centre
Calle San Pedro
MARINA
SPAIN
HENDAYE
ramp
FERRY
cantina de Guadalupe
OLD TOWN
FRANCE
AIRPORT
HONDARRIBIA
Ace hill walks
BIARRITZ AIRPORT
OLAIA
DONOSTIA -
SAN SEBASTIAN
BIDASOA
IRUN
JAIZKIBEL
N
W
E
S
Hallatt
(Not to scale in any way.)

If you are visiting Hondarribia, your first stop should be the super helpful tourist information centre in Arma Plaza at the very top of the old town (or there is another one out towards the boat marina). They speak English very well (or will endure your bad Spanish) and have free maps of the town and information on what is happening. They also sell tickets to things like the Basque sport of Jai Alai. Opening hours are similar to most shops, except they don't have a siesta break.

Hondarribia is in the region of Gipuzkoa and about 10 miles away from its capital of Donostia-San Sebastian, but happens to host its airport (EAS). It abuts Irun, its more workaday neighbour, which has local and national train stations as well as a myriad of small shops and chain stores.

PUBLIC TRANSPORT

Public transport in this part of Spain is, in a word, awesome. A half hour bus trip will cost you about 3 euros and about half that if you get yourself a MUGI card. Go into the stationary shop almost opposite the E21 bus stop by the roundabout to buy a card for 5 euros and add money to it to charge it up. You can recharge cards at the tobacconist opposite the bakery-café, Amona Margarita. The card covers public transport in Gipuzkoa and you can use it on local trains (the "topo", or mole) that run from Hendaye and Irun to Donostia and along the coast. The topo goes as far as Bilbao and isn't fast, but it is a fun trip. RENFE trains go from Hendaye, Irun, or Donostia to all major towns in Spain.

If you want to get to Bilbao fast (including the airport), there is a bus that goes from Donostia and is operated by PESA. It is more expensive than the train (17 euros at time of writing), but is at least twice as fast.

More information on MUGI, buses and trains:

http://www.mugi.eus

http://ekialdebus.eus

http://www.pesa.net

http://www.euskotren.eus

There is something about boardwalks that makes even industrial estates attractive.

SHOPPING, HEALTH AND FITNESS

This is our local store, where Duncan buys Diet Coke and cocktail mix, I buy tomatoes and anchovies and Billie gets scratches though dogs aren't really allowed in.

Hallatt

15

Most of Hondarribia's shops are small, independent and quite traditional, supplying all the basics. There are a multitude of butchers, bakers and greengrocers. There are five fish shops in town and the quality is superb, as they are supplied by the boats that come into the town port, as well as from further afield. Solbes is a local chain of good food stores and sells great meat and cheese and a good selection of wine. There is more great wine (though often more expensive) at Route 33.

If you need more variety, or to get international ingredients like spices, coconut milk, or decent chocolate, Donostia-San Sebastian is a better bet. Alternatively, you can brave the behemoth Al Campo megastore in the Txingudi shopping centre (which can be reached by bus).

MARKETS

The town has a local growers' market on a Wednesday morning, outside the south gate of the old town, near Bar Larra. It sells mostly vegetables, with some fruit and eggs. The bread comes from the Amona Margarita bakery. The same market moves to Calle San Pedro on Saturday mornings.

Irun merits a visit on a Saturday for its outdoor market (Mercado de Urbanibia), which has good value local produce, as well as standard market stall tatt.

The best local food market on a Saturday is in Hendaye, close to where the ferry comes in. This market has a better variety of meat, great bread, excellent cheese and some good produce from local growers. It's weird having to switch to French, but many of the stallholders speak Spanish, which is lucky, as our schoolday French is abysmal.

LENDABISICO ECHEA

This shop sells a mix of hardware, hats and who-knows what in drawers labelled "NO TOCAR" with a skull to make it clear. 💀

Hallatt

HEALTH

A friend told us that, in negotiating a peace agreement with the Basque nationalists, the federal government made many concessions, one of which was to fund healthcare at a much higher level than in the rest of Spain. I've also read that the Basque Government collects its own taxes and returns only 10% of those to central government. It chooses how to spend the rest and healthcare benefits from that. Whatever the funding situation is, Hondarribia has tip top health facilities, though the nearest emergency hospital is down the road in Irun.

The European Health Insurance Card (EHIC), for EU residents, covers emergency healthcare in Spain, but it might also cover regular healthcare in the Basque Country.

One time I had to go to the health centre in Hondarribia. I presented my passport and EHIC to the administrators on the ground floor and made an appointment for a couple of days later to see a doctor on the first floor who approved a blood test for my iron levels... on the ground floor. It was back to the administrators to make an appointment for the test. Weirdly, it was for 8.17am. When I turned up for that, you could see why, because the system ran like clockwork, lining up at one door to check in to be shunted to another door to go in to see one of the four phlebotomists who were taking blood. After giving blood, you exited out of another door and were done. I made another appointment to see the doctor for a week after that, got the results (fine) and waited for someone to charge me something. I never got a bill and still don't know why.

Dentistry is mostly private, as in the UK, but check ups were much cheaper, running at between 30 to 50 euros, depending on X-rays, time to clean, etc.

In the winter months, the local growers' market has less and less to sell. Eventually, there's little more than potatoes, leafy greens and leeks. Still good.

Hallatt

19

FITNESS

The best exercise in Hondarribia is free and outside, with the river, beach and surrounding hills providing lots of opportunity to kayak, paddle, swim, surf, walk, bike, or run. But sometimes the weather doesn't play ball and you can go to the "polideportivo" to play it there instead. As well as racquet sports, there is a 25 metre pool. I used the pool in the winter and paid about 85 euros to get a "bono" ticket to swim 20 times. Entry includes a sauna and a jacuzzi and the whole complex was a lot cleaner than many of the facilities I had experienced in the UK. Most people actually use the showers before swimming, and everyone has to wear a swimming hat in the pool and flip flops around it.

For information on accommodation and banking, head to June (which is not a good time to arrive to look for accommodation in the Basque Country).

The Basques aren't as obsessed with health & safety as the English. That's a good thing. Most of the time.

BASQUE - EUSKARA

We learned a few words of Basque, but not many and you really don't need to learn many to be polite. As Basques will readily admit, Euskara (the Basque language) is fiendishly difficult to learn. We have friends who have lived in the Basque Country for a decade or more who haven't been able to learn it and one of them teaches English, Spanish and French!

There are a few Basque words and phrases that will take you a long way:

Eskerrik asko (eskerrickasko) - thank you. As a tourist, this will score you big points and get you better service in restaurants (especially if you have taught your 6 year old niece to say it to the waitress).

Kaixo (ki-show) - hi. Another Basque hello you might hear is "aupa". You can always use the Spanish "hola" or "buenos dias/buenas tardes", but these Basque greetings work well with people you know, or in less formal situations like walking in the hills.

Agur (a very sing-songy aggooor) - goodbye. This is my absolute favourite, as it is like the Mexican wave of Euskara. If someone is leaving somewhere like a shop and they say "agur", complete strangers in the shop will join in with "agur", in farewell to this person they've never met. Basques are very friendly saying "goodbye".

If you want to learn more Basque, there are some great online sources (see Further Reading). For the purposes of this book, I've used Basque words where they are commonly used, but otherwise Spanish.

NB. When talking about "Spanish" in the Basque Country, it is polite to call it "Castellano", as it is a language that isn't accepted by all of Spain (e.g. In Catalunya they are switching more and more to Catalan). That said, many Basques who want independence don't even consider the Basque Country to be part of Spain.

It seems that a lot of older women in town shop at the same clothing store. I like to think it is called "Black Widow".

JANUARY - URTARRILA

Dogs aren't allowed on Hondarribia beach in any season, but in winter everyone ignores the signs.

We didn't notice much happening on New Year's Day, but on the 2nd of January there was a random parade of the "gigantes" (giants made of papier mâché) around the old town. It might have a been a practice run for the parade of the Three Kings on the 5th, when it really kicks off. Hondarribia is thronged with families, whose kids go nuts trying to catch as many caramellos (sweets), thrown from the people in the parade, as they can. The parade is fairly low key compared to Donostia-San Sebastian, which is packed with people and has genuine black people as the kings (painfully on the first Twelfth Night that we were there, Hondarribians blacked-up to portray the three kings, even though there were black people who live in the town. They insisted that if those black people wanted to take part in the parade, they would be welcome. It was great to see a black guy did take part the following year, so things are changing, little by little).

It is in January that the cold weather sets in. We didn't see snow in Hondarribia, but it sometimes dusted the hills that circle the town. The sea normally keeps the temperatures above freezing, at a time when the interior of Spain can be mighty frosty. During our second winter we had a few days when it dipped below zero and we skirted sheets of ice walking to the café in the morning. But that was when it reached 20 below zero in other parts of the country, so we counted ourselves lucky. Whenever it wasn't raining, we made the most of the surrounding hills to go walking.

There is a fantastic walk from Hondarribia to Pasajes de San Juan (Pasaia Donibane). This is where Victor Hugo spent a few days, meriting a whole little museum dedicated to him. It's free and well worth a look. The walk goes along much of the stunning coastline and takes in a part of the ridge of Jaizkibel. I walked in the other direction with a friend and warned her that the signs said it took 7 hours to do. Unlike on some of the walks we've done, when they say 7 hours, they mean 7 hours of actual walking, not 7 hours of walking with stops to eat, drink, or admire the view. In the end it took us 9 hours with lots of stopping. We didn't take a map, as the day was clear and the walk is well-signposted, with lots of red and white blazes painted on trees, rocks, or actual signs. Apart from the steep ascent out of Pasajes, it isn't a particularly demanding, or technical walk. But 7 hours of walking takes its toll and I was glad to have

those walking poles that make you look like a prat, but take the repeated stress off your joints. My friend had to use them for the last half hour and, when we hobbled into Hondarribia, we had a therapeutic paddle in the sea and then a much more therapeutic beer, before continuing home.

We often did the best section of this walk by parking in the forest near the bar of Justiz (as you are driving up the hill from Hondarribia, you look for signs to Justiz and the driving range on the right. The car park is in the clearing to the right just after this.). You walk past the forest through pasture to the spectacular rocky coastline, along and then up a road to Justiz, where you can stop for a drink before doing the last hill to get back to the car.

TAMBORRADA

From midnight to midnight on the 20th January, Donostia celebrates its patron saint's day by going nuts about drumming. It's been happening since 1836 and has evolved to be a huge display of percussive madness. For 24 hours, more than 125 companies of drummers play to traditional tunes through the streets and on the beaches of the city. Each company wears a uniform and has 20 to 50 drums, together with brass bands, flag-bearers and water-carriers. It seems to be like 8th September in Hondarribia, when men like dressing up as soldiers. With this one there is a little less shooting and a lot more drumming.

FEBRUARY - OTSAILA

There are three sets of outdoor escalators in Hondarribia. This is amazing, as it rains here nearly as much as in England.

Hallatt

Wind and rain and lots of it, seemed to be the weather for the month of February when we were there, but just as we were getting sick of it, we were surprised by spells of sunshine and calm. Though temperatures are often mild (10 to 12 degrees and occasionally almost 20), the weather is often wild, with winter storms toppling trees and looking as if they might wrench roofs from the buildings. That didn't happen in Hondarribia, though it did in other parts of northern Spain.

Tortilla Individual

Hallatt

The lengthening days give you hope and, as we walked along the river bank to our morning coffee, we would often see the sun rise over the French mountains. When the weather did break, it was good to stretch the legs and tick off another walk from our book of Hondarribian walking maps. We'd often stop off at the Cantina de Guadalupe for lunch, or at Errandonea to have a beer and a little tortilla.

CARNIVAL

Towards the end of the month, the Catholic calendar ramps up for Lent. In England, we have Shrove Tuesday, known as Pancake Day in our heathen household, but Spain goes the whole hog with Carnival. Though the word seems to have its root in the saying goodbye to "carne", or meat, the original meaning was probably pagan, as many of the festivities in the Lent lead up are definitely older than the Catholic church in Spain.

Each town has its own way of celebrating Carnival. In Hondarribia, there is a procession of hundreds of people in various floats, dancing groups and bands. People were dressed up as medieval torturers, superheroes, bikers, World War II dancers.... anything. There was no logic to it - it was just an excuse to dress up, dance, play music really loud and drink. Some paraders carried hip flasks to stave off the inclement weather and the rest braved it until the end when they piled into the town's bars to warm up and get wasted. All of it was good humoured, as always.

The first Carnival festival in the country is celebrated in Ituren, in the Basque Country. We went to it and there is nothing Christian about it. It actually happened on the last weekend of January and was quite a spectacle for such a small village of 200 or so inhabitants. To begin with, the Joaldunak walk around the village and between it and the neighbouring village of Zubieta. We'd seen these guys with the bells on their bums previously, in Hondarribia. Their purpose is to scare away witches. It seems to work. The Joaldunak and a marching band go from bar to bar and stop for a drink and a pincho before moving on. This part is very traditional and has been happening for centuries, I'm sure.

But after this, it went very crazy. Local lads dressed up in the ugliest costumes possible (crazy clowns, prostitutes, hunters draped in offal) and ran around with buzzing chainsaws (thankfully with chains removed) and corpses of foxes, or boars. Some of them raced up and down the streets in beat up cars, or mopeds, that would never pass any inspection. It was raucous and aggressive and we were told it was a fairly recent addition to the proceedings. Later we found out that the council has banned the use of dead animals for future carnivals. Yay.

MARCH - MARTXOA

Amona Margarita is part of our daily routine. There are great baked goods and coffee, but the best thing is the people. There's the old lady who gives me fresh anchovies and tries to give our dog jamon. There's the nice man & his daughter who has the friendly puppy. But mostly, there are just so many friends.

Hallatt

Spring gets into gear as the days lengthen and the sun becomes more powerful. There are yellow primroses and celandines on the walk up to Jaizkibel and the town council has to start cutting the grass around the old town walls.

We like to go out a lot with our dog, Billie, but the March mornings and evenings were still cool and not ideal for sitting outside. Fortunately, Hondarribia was one of the most dog-friendly towns we encountered in our travels through Spain. Although most restaurants prohibit dogs, Billie was allowed in most bars, even in the bar of the Michelin-starred Alameda. Our regular coffee spot, sourdough bakery and wi-fi haven, Amona Margarita, was also dog-friendly.

As we spent more time in the town, Billie made friends with more people. We had to stop the stern, but lovely old lady, Juanita from feeding him croissants and jamón in the café. He would be beckoned into the local shop for scratches and even as far as the kitchen of Bar Zabala for bacon. The nice lady at the preserved meats shop in Calle San Pedro nearly always threw Billie a piece of salami, or chorizo. Billie thought Hondarribia was the best place he had ever lived.

TXOTX

I grew up in the West Country of the UK and retain a love of cider. There are two areas of Spain that also have a big cider culture. One is in Asturias, where the cider is like the flat scrumpy that I'm used to (though a little less strong and slightly sweeter). The other is in the Basque Country. Here the cider is completely natural, around 6% alcohol, flat and quite acidic. It's an acquired taste, and one of the best places to acquire it is at a txotx at a cider house (sagardotegi).

The txotx season runs during the winter months of January to April. After fermentation, but before the cider is put into bottles, they pour the cider directly from the barrels. The txotx has evolved to include a traditional menu of salt cod omelette; cod with peppers; char-grilled T-bone steaks; and Idiazábal cheese, quince jelly and walnuts. Because you are filling your glass so frequently (to the call of "txotx!"), you often eat standing at a tall table. This set menu costs around 30 euros and includes as much cider as you can drink.

MACKEREL SEASON

Duncan isn't keen on them, but if you are like me and like oily fish (or pescado azul - blue fish - as they call them in Spain), March is a great time, as it is the start of blue fish season. There is a quota of mackerel that can be caught and it seems that the boats race to meet it. They bring in so much of it that it is sold off very cheaply. This is despite quotas being cut in recent years, so much so that the catch might only last a couple of weeks. I might have missed it had our friend, Javier, not given me mackerel caught by his son-in-law.

Mackerel season is followed by anchovy season. Juanita's son was also a fisherman and Juanita would give a lot of the fish he gave her to me. That meant more anchovies than I could eat. I tried to fillet them and preserve them in vinegar, but though okay, they were never as good as the fine boquerones that you can buy in the local shop. Billie and I ate a lot of blue fish in March.

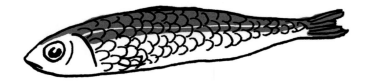

APRIL - APIRILA

Towards the sports centre there is a wall with some scenes carved into stone. My favourite is the one with the confused owl.

Hallatt

40

The hills are covered in the acid green of spring. Eating a menu del dia outside in the sun, it is warm enough to be in short sleeves, but I found it too cold to be in the sea without a wetsuit.

MUTRIKU'S FIESTA DE VERDEL

Though mackerel season was finished in Hondarribia, it was far from over down the coast. Mutriku is a little fishing village that has got around the problem of early mackerel excess by making a day of it. After I read about it, we had to go. I was prepared for the usual Spanish fiesta day craziness, so we drove over early and arrived at about 9.30. The village was practically deserted. We walked from the car park, through the old, narrow streets, out past the port and seawater pools to the massive breakwater that faced the ocean. Nothing. We went back into town, pottered around and found the tourist information office. I asked whether there was a mackerel festival.

"Yes," said the friendly woman behind the desk.

"Where is it?"

"Right here, in the centre."

I assumed that, in true English style, we must have arrived way too early. "When does it start?"

"In about five minutes," she answered and, as we stepped back out, we saw that crowds were appearing out of nowhere. The bars opened and the fiesta began. Everyone was putting out trays and trays of free mackerel pinchos. They must have been good, because Duncan ate half a dozen of them.

The following year we went back and stayed the night. We discovered even more bars than the year before. They also set up stalls with cheap beer and mackerel for the evening. There was live music, which we managed to miss, being distracted by the great atmosphere in all the bars in the old town. Though the music and mackerel stalls in the harbour get packed up early, the rest of the town keeps on partying. People were still out when we got up the next day and the café above the town square was full of young men with their last drink of the night, as we had our first coffee of the day.

Hondarribia's Easter Parade

Hallalt

It was the first Saturday in April the two years that we went, but you can check on the town website: www.mutriku.eus.

EASTER

Most of the Iberian peninsula goes a bit crazy in the run up to Easter and Hondarribia is no exception. There is a parade from the paroquia (the Church of Our Lady of the Assumption) which starts with the Descent of Christ from the Cross. Not the real Christ, obviously. And they aren't real Roman soldiers escorting Christ, as I'm pretty sure that Romans wouldn't have been wearing Day-Glo pink long-johns, though I could be wrong. And there is more. The procession includes men dressed up as monks and apostles and all of them carrying various effigies of religious celebrities. They walk around the old town with their cargo, blazing torches and candles, accompanied by a marching band.

OPILA

As well as the various church ceremonies and parades, there is a cake that appears in every bakery around the end of April called an Opila. To us, it didn't seem anything special - a sponge cake with some eggs on top. Real eggs too, not Cadbury's Mini Eggs. We had a small slice of it and again, it just tasted like sponge cake. But people pay more than 25 euros for one of these! Further questioning of folks in the know (the people who work at Amona Margarita) confirmed that it was just a cake made locally that people pick up to take out to the countryside and eat. The tradition started with godparents giving their godchildren the cake on the day of San Marcos (April 25th), to be blessed in church before being enjoyed by the family. However, with older children, the cake is often accompanied by a lot of alcohol and the excursion can become a bit of a party. So much so that the local schools frown upon the practice, as the Opila day often disrupts the school week. Kids head to the hills to party with cake and kalimotxo (a mix of coca cola and red wine). I still don't understand why the cake costs nearly 30 euros.

MAY – MAIATZA

The sea may not have warmed up much, but May is usually a great time to be out and enjoying the better weather and the longer days. We did a lot of travelling in May, going out to Asturias and Galicia one year and returning to Asturias the next. Asturias was the only region in Spain that came close to the Basque Country in our affections, but it is said to be cursed with worse weather. Unlike the interior, the northern coast of Spain is very green, but this comes at the cost of a lot more rain.

BASQUE FOOD CULTURE

The cooler climate brings the Spanish tourists and retirees to the Basque Country in summer. Many are also attracted by the food culture. Travelling around other parts of Spain made us realise how good Basque food is and how much it suits our way of eating. Eating times are shifted about an hour ahead of the UK at lunch (which means you are eating at the same time, as most kitchens open at around 1pm, vs. 12pm in the UK). People tend to have dinner around 8 or 9pm. Further south, the Spanish eat much later, making lunch closer to 2pm onwards and dinner from 9 or 10pm. This kills me, as I am not a night owl. But not only are the Basque hours better, the Basque culture of pinchos on the bar means that if you feel like eating at 6 or 7 o'clock, you can. We found it suited us (and was a lot more affordable), to have a big lunch and then a few pinchos with some drinks in the evening.

Menu del dias range from 10 to 30 euros and nearly always include three courses, bread and a drink (sometimes a whole bottle of wine). It is a great way to eat a variety of affordable food and to eat in season. I found that this was the best means of finding vegetable dishes. The Basques are big fans of beans, chick peas and non-hot peppers. There is nearly always some kind of seafood dish and there will always be meat courses. After you have had a menu del dia, you can see why the siesta is popular. It also means you don't need the more expensive sit-down meal at night and can just graze pinchos from bar to bar with a few drinks, until you've had enough.

One of the oldest
buildings in
Hondarribia.
Not one
straight
line.

If you do want a sit-down meal, a lot of the restaurants serve the same thing and you will often find the following on the menu, usually as large, or half serves (raciones, or medio raciones) :

- Ensalada mixta — lettuce, tomato, onion, boiled egg, tuna and white asparagus
- Pimientos con bacalao — salt cod-stuffed peppers
- Squid, either as deep-fried calamares, cooked in their ink, or simply grilled (txipirones/ chipirones are small squid and they are the best!)
- Pimientos de padrón — flash-fried green peppers
- Pulpo — octopus, tenderised, usually grilled and always expensive
- Plates of jamón ibérico
- Grilled or breaded meat: pork (e.g. lomo, which is tenderloin) and veal (ternera) are popular and lamb (cordero) and beef (e.g. the often excellent chuletón) are rarer
- And a variety of fish and shellfish

A phrasebook is helpful when you first arrive, especially if it covers seafood. The merluza (hake) is usually cheap and excellent and the mussels (mejillones) are nearly as good as in France.

TXOKOS – SOCIEDADES

The txokos, or cooking clubs, are a feature of the Basque Country and said to be the source of the rich food heritage and all-star chefs. They used to be the domain of men, but now most are friendly to women and children (though rarely to dogs). To visit them you need to find someone who is a member. Our first such visit was thanks to friends of Duncan's Spanish teacher, who are members of the one down by the boat marina. Each txoko works on a cooperative basis, with members chipping in dues to buy supplies of basic cooking ingredients and drinks, in bulk. When members cook, they bring the other ingredients they need and then write up the communal ingredients that they use on a tab. At the end of the meal, the tab is counted up, shared and paid for. It is like a massive honesty box and it seems to work. Txokos are a great way to get out of the house, socialise and have a good meal on the cheap.

Pulpo

Hallatt

JUNE - EKAINA

The weather was pleasant for us in June, with not much rain and temperatures usually in the low to mid 20s.

As summer begins in earnest, the outdoor events pop up around the town. You can get a listing of what's happening up at the information centre in Arma Plaza, but that doesn't cover everything. Even living by Gipuzkoa Square, we often wouldn't know that there was going to be a concert there until the events guys started setting up the stage. It could be anything from a local choir singing Basque songs, to a brass band from the Netherlands playing big band renditions of Abba. And it was always free.

MEDIEVAL FESTIVAL

When we first arrived in Hondarribia it was a weekend in mid June and the medieval old town looked VERY medieval, with crowds of people dressed like peasants, flags and a portcullis on the gateway of the bridge that leads in to the massive old town wall. It turned out to be a medieval festival that was going on all weekend. It's a fun time to be in the old town. The centre is cleared of all the cars and is taken over by produce and artisan stalls, medieval decorations, giant puppets and people dressed up as if they are on the set of Game of Thrones. You can watch a bit of blacksmithing, or carpentry, or mock fights (at least I think they were). There are also musical performances, dancing and demonstrations of falconry and whatever you call messing about with other birds of prey. As if that weren't enough, the Wheels and Waves festival came to town so that the medieval cosplayers were joined by bikers, who strangely didn't look out of place.

BONFIRE MADNESS

On the 23rd June, as the sun sets, the townspeople light masses of bonfires around the town and on the beaches in celebration of St John's Eve (the day of St John the Baptist being on the 24th). It is another example of a Christian festival being a little bit pagan, as the date falls around the solstice. It is customary to write down the things that are bothering you in your life and throw them into the fire so that they will be consumed. Worth a try.

The old town in Hondarribia dates back to medieval times and is still surrounded by an impressive wall.

This part is like a fairytale castle turret. That smells of wee.

FINDING ACCOMMODATION IN THE SUMMER

Initially, we stayed in an AirBnB place in the old town. We had rented it for a month, thinking that would give us time to organise something more permanent, but it was a crazy time of year to be looking for accommodation. It turns out that everyone wants to be in Hondarribia in the summer months. Madrileños and others from the dry, hot centre have their holidays here and rental accommodation is as rare as hens' teeth. The first agency we went into told us (quite rudely) that we wouldn't find anything. Luckily, the next place we went into (A M Sorolla) was a lot more friendly. They said there were two flats we could rent for more than just the summer and less than 1000 euros. We agreed to rent one of them. We read the contract, understood about half of it, and signed it. It all worked out fine.

BANKING AND BIKING

In order to pay for our flat and the ensuing bills, we had to set up a local bank account. We went with Santander because they have branches all over the country and we thought it would be easier. They are also one of the most expensive banks around. Just getting an ATM card cost 28 euros! Transactions that would be free in the UK cost a few euros. We made the mistake of having them set up the monthly payments and were charged 4 euros each time one went out. If we had set them up ourselves online, they would have been free. From what we have heard, the local Kutxa banks are a lot cheaper, but don't have wide coverage outside of the Basque Country. You have to weigh up how much you will need to use a bank when travelling and how much you will need it at home.

Once we had our accommodation and bank account sorted, I was able to relax and enjoy the prospect of the long summer ahead of us. I looked for a second hand bicycle to buy. Now the Spanish don't have a great culture of second hand goods, so it was a challenge. eBay was a dead end (and not great for trying out bicycles) and we didn't then know about the second hand sanctuary of Emaus in Irun. Someone at Amona Margarita suggested I try Higer, a two-wheeler shop and garage in the Marina. That's where I found Petunia. She was pink, old and had clearly seen better days, but she had once been a quality bike. The guy wanted 95 euros for her, which was over the odds, but we settled on 90. I got my money's worth because every time I had any little problem, he fixed her for free.

Like many old ladies, Petunia wasn't very good at hills. Her gearing was very high and she would change up if you stood up on the pedals. Her brakes weren't great going downhill and were almost useless in the wet. But most of the places I wanted to get to - the beach, the port, Irun - were on the flat, and I try not to cycle in the rain, so she worked out well for the couple of years we were there. Cycling is a popular pastime in Spain and drivers give you a lot of room on the roads. It would be fun to have a good bike and cycle up into the hills around Jaizkibel.

JULY — UZTAILA

Though it can rain at any time of year in the Basque Country, we were lucky with the weather in July. It was usually hot (high 20s to 30s) and dry and perfect for hitting the beaches. Unlike in other parts of Spain, it is rarely suffocatingly hot.

CIDER DAY - SAGARDO EGUNA

Around the middle of July, there is a cider festival in Gipuzkoa Square in Hondarribia. For 5 euros, you get a glass that you can fill up as often as you like (though it is bad form to actually fill it - you want to put in a couple of inches at most). The admission price also includes a pincho of either chistorra (like a mild, skinny chorizo), or tortilla (the potato and onion Spanish omelette), though given the amount of cider on offer, it is worth going back to buy more pinchos. The square is surrounded by big barrels of cider, manned by the producers who release streams of it to land in your glass. You need to catch it low, move the glass up and move away as the next person comes in behind you with their glass. Catching the cider low and having it spatter on the glass mixes in air, which improves the flavour. Needless to say, there is an art to the cider pour that we never mastered.

BLUES FESTIVAL

We were in Hondarribia for the 9th, 10th and 11th Blues Festivals. The festival is held towards the end of July (the date depends on when the Running of the Bulls is happening in Pamplona, as they don't like to clash) and it is massive. There is a huge stage near the ferry terminal down in the Marina, a smaller stage in Calle San Pedro and a mid-sized one up in the old town in Arma Plaza. It takes days to set up (and pack up) the stages and the concession stands. The organisers bring in bands from all over the world. It must cost a small fortune to put on and they don't charge anything for you to go to the concerts. It's insane and a friend of ours has said that it might not continue for too much longer. Hondarribia council seems to have a lot of money, but we can't see how they can afford to keep paying for this festival without someone else dipping into their pockets to help. Their only sponsor seems to be Carlsberg and there has been resistance from local businesses to cough up any local sponsorship.

25TH JULY: KUTXA (BOX) DAY

Our friends in Amona Margarita tried to explain this festival to us the first year and, because our Spanish wasn't very good, we thought we had mistranslated it. They seemed to be telling us that a woman would parade with a box on her head, accompanied by fishermen, from the big church to the archway of the Brotherhood of the Fishermen. But this is exactly what happened. What we ended up calling "The Procession of the Woman With the Box on Her Head" is actually known as the "Kutxa Entrega (or Handing Over of the Box)". We were close. The box contains fishermen's papers and when the woman (a daughter of a fisherman) reaches the archway of the Cofradia, accompanied by the fishermen and a marching band, she spins around and around to bring prosperity to the fishermen. It was one of my favourite fiestas.

SAN SEBASTIAN JAZZ FESTIVAL

Donostia-San Sebastian has its jazz festival in the third week of July and it is worth going, if only for all the free outdoor concerts and great atmosphere.

La Hermandad de Pescadores is a great restaurant, with a long building, that wouldn't fit in this drawing, so I cheated. The archway on the left is where the procession of the woman-with-the-box-on-her-head ends up. She spins around there to bring luck to the fishermen.

Hallatt

AUGUST – ABUZTUA

The ferry that runs between Hondarribia and Hendaye is packed in the summer with people going to France for the beach and Spain for the food.

Hallatt

Sometimes hot, sometimes wet and always packed with tourists.

August is not the best time to come to Hondarribia, as the French are on holiday en masse and at times Calle San Pedro is so full of people, it is hard to walk down the street, let alone find a spot to have a drink and a pincho. Getting the ferry to and from France means queuing and sometimes you have to wait for a couple of boats to fill up before you get on board.

If you are here, you can avoid the crowds and go to the calm town beach before 11 and leave as the crowds arrive at midday. I went to the surf beach in Hendaye by paddling across the river with my body board or stand up paddle board. But for the best swims, the locals head down to the far end of Hondarribia, at the port. Though this is a working harbour, with fishing boats offloading their catch for local stores, restaurants and beyond, you are still able to access the port wall (unlike other parts of the world where we have lived, where they have used the flimsy excuse of terrorism to make the port off limits to the public). People swim from the breakwater and the first year, I used to swim around the giant buoys that the fishing boats moor at. Or I would walk on to the rocky beach of Playa de los Frailes (beach of the monks), where the crystal clear water was very inviting on calm days. The next year, I discovered the super-local spot on the other side of the port wall. You can jump off the breakwater concrete blocks into deep water and swim to Playa de los Frailes (it takes about 20 minutes, if the current isn't against you). And there is a freshwater spring that is piped out of the breakwater that you can shower with. A wild swim with all mod cons!

Dogs aren't allowed on the beaches in the summer, though are tolerated at the little river beach near the ferry, as long as there aren't lots of kids there. Further up the river, you can find boat ramps where you can take your dog in. If it hasn't rained for a while and the tide isn't so low that all the sharp oyster shell-encrusted rocks are exposed, it is a lovely place to swim from. And around high tide, you can jump into the water from the boat jetty, if you have the nerve.

PIL-PIL

On August 15, the day of the Assumption, there is a salt cod with pil-pil contest, held on the grass to the south of the old town wall. Pil-pil is a classic Basque emulsified sauce that is hard to make, so this is the place to watch and learn!

BASQUE SPORTS

A lot of Basque sport seems to involve showing how macho a man is. Lifting really heavy rocks and using sharp axes to chop a massive log the competitor is standing on, are two of them. Something that looks a little more approachable, but which is just as difficult, to master is jai alai, or cesta punta. Through the summer months, you can pay 12 euros to watch games between various local teams of two. It's like a crazy game of squash, with a ball about twice the size, but a court that is more than four times the length. To make things just that little

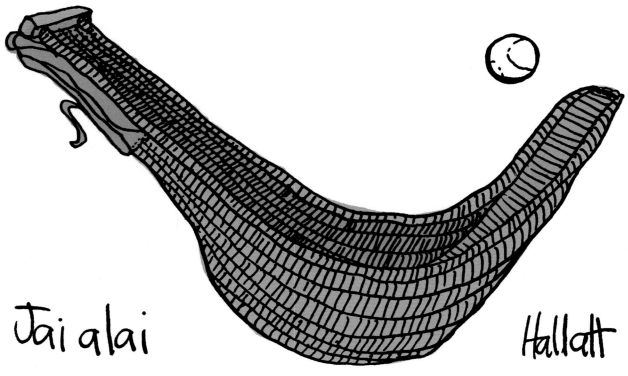

Jai alai

Hallatt

bit trickier, the players don't use racquets, rather long skinny baskets that wrap around their wrists to form an extension of their arms. As well as a very entertaining match, the entry price includes a classic Basque dish of marmitako, which is a tuna stew. They throw in a free glass of wine, or two, too.

Another tough sport that you can watch in the summer is the rowing. Every weekend, the teams assemble in one of the coastal towns for an event that lasts about an hour. There is widespread support for the Hondarribia team in our town. Unfortunately, the team colours are an ugly shade of green, but that doesn't put off every man and his dog (and our dog) wearing it.

On the day that the race came to Hondarribia, people were massed on the beach, along the breakwater and in dozens of boats out in the harbour. The long wooden boats used by the competitors have evolved from the whaling boats the Basques used to use to row out in the open ocean. The regattas are usually easier to see on TV than from the shore, but if you do turn up to watch in person, you should make the most of the barbecue. Regatta season is also tuna season and big hunks of it get served up as very affordable pinchos.

SEPTEMBER - IRAILA

Often one of the most pleasant months, with settled, sunny weather and warm, clear water for swimming and surfing.

PARTY TIME IN HONDARRIBIA

Every town in the Basque Country has their fiesta day. In Hondarribia, it is the 8th September, the day of the Virgin of Guadalupe (which is also the name of the church that overlooks Hondarribia from the ridge near the range of Jaizkibel). On this day in 1638, the town broke a 69 day siege by 27,000 French troops. It is celebrated with the Alarde, which is a quasi-military procession, performed (mainly) by the men of the town.

This is a very macho festival. The men march in companies, carrying the traditional whistles (most commonly the txibilito), drums, or guns (we don't know whether they are all live rounds, but at least some of them are. One year someone was killed when they were shot on a balcony. This hasn't stopped them.). A token woman is selected by each company, sort of like an individual contender for Miss Basque Country. They don't have to be pretty (though they usually are), but they do have to be considered the sweetest girl around. The women do not march. Except that is starting to change. There is one mixed company, which has not been well received. We saw them march and didn't see any hostility, but we were told that they are often booed by the crowds. The march takes the companies around the town all morning and then up to the Virgin of Guadalupe for a midday ceremony.

Although the 8th is the main day, the town is in fiesta mode pretty much all week. The compañias, or regiments (representing each of the town's neighbourhoods), practise their marching, whistling and drumming around the streets and it feels like you are hearing the same tunes over and over and over again. But for the locals, it is a very evocative time. The tunes are unique to the area and are taught from father to son. The celebrations culminate on the 10th with a mass held in memory of those who died in the siege of 1638.

After the madness of the Alarde, Hondarribia calms down and enjoys the quiet warm days of the rest of the month. Most of the tourists have gone and it is a great time to relax in the town and make the most of the beaches.

During the last week of September, Donostia-San Sebastian has its film festival.

67

October - Urria

olive

anchovy

guindilla
pickled
pepper
(only a
bit hot)

The Gilda is named after Rita Hayworth's character in the film of the same name.

Hallatt

The mild autumn weather continues in October, with cool nights. In our first year, it was crazy hot during the day and we had to seek shade to eat out. In the second year, it was cooler, but still pleasant. We had stretches of dry weather and stretches of wet, but you can always stand out under an awning and enjoy the pinchos in Calle San Pedro.

PINCHOS (PINTXOS IN BASQUE) – THE BASQUE TAPAS

Tapas are a feature of bars everywhere in Spain. In some places (like Leon, and Granada), tapas come free with your drinks. Often (though not always) the drinks are more expensive to cover the cost of the tapas. In the Basque Country, you don't get a free pincho, but you do get a choice and the choice is incredible.

Pinchos on the bar are usually very good value, between 1.50 and 2.50 euros. They range from the "Gilda" (spicy pickled guindilla peppers with olives and a marinated anchovy) to pulpo (octopus) with smoked salmon and caramelised onions.

You usually pay more for pinchos that are cooked to order, but these can be good value too, as you often get something more substantial than a morsel of food on top of a piece of bread. The bar, Ardoka does things like fried artichokes with jamón, or entrecôte with green peppers.

Unfortunately, many Basque bars rely on a lot of foie gras to beef up the flavour of their more sophisticated pinchos, which doesn't appeal if you care at all about animal welfare. The same can be said if you investigate where a lot of the pork products come from, as the Spanish raise many of their pigs inside, which is not much of a life. According to Hamazing.com,

"...The Bellota pig is completely free range and organic, leaving it with much better developed muscles and a stress-free life which naturally produces a healthier, more tender and more flavoursome meat. ... The Recebo and the Cebo de Campo would be second on the ladder in the free-range and organic world, with Cebo being the bottom rung of the ibérico ladder. It's probably worth mentioning that around 99% of all serrano pigs are factory farmed and fed on processed foodstuffs."

Ref: http://www.hamazing.com/articles/spanish-jamon-iberico-a-guide-to-choosing-the-best-iberian-ham-from-spain/

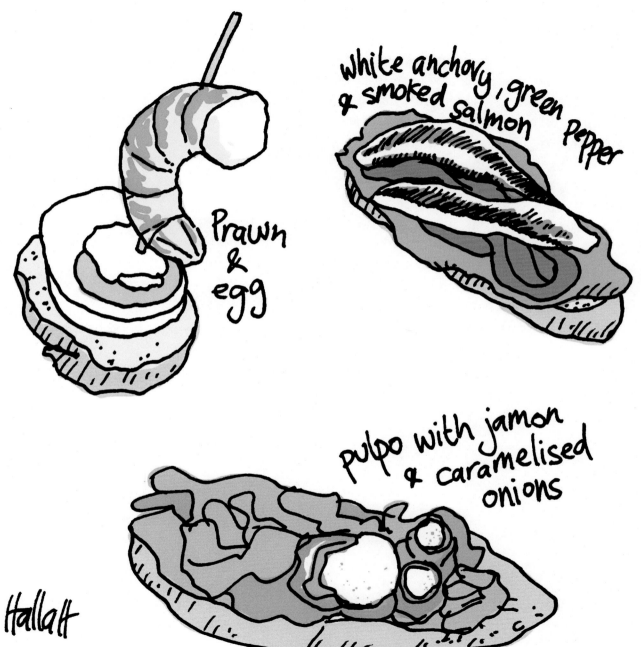

Prawn & egg

white anchovy, green pepper & smoked salmon

pulpo with jamon & caramelised onions

Hallatt

AUTUMN HARVEST

October is a time when the local markets are going strong, with plenty of produce, such as peppers, beans, courgettes, aubergines and squashes, swamping the tables. Tomatoes don't grow well in the area because the humidity causes a lot of fungal problems. If you do see tomatoes, they will almost certainly have been sprayed with a copper-based fungicide. Tinges of green around the stalks are a giveaway and, if that doesn't put you off, you should wash the tomatoes thoroughly before eating.

Some things that won't have been sprayed are mushrooms, because they will have been collected from the local hillsides. Mushroom-hunting is a favourite Basque pastime and the fruits of this appear in the markets, especially in the Autumn months. We went out looking for mushrooms ourselves, but didn't come home with much because we are terrified of poisoning ourselves. We can only confidently identify three edible mushrooms and only found one of them (a cep, or penny bun). So the markets are a great resource.

THE BOINA/TXAPELA

As the weather cools, you could consider picking up a Basque beret. Some of the best are made in Tolosa, by Elósegu (www.boinaselosegui.com) and are readily available in shops in Hondarribia, like the souvenir shop in Gipuzkoa Square. The difficulty is working out how to wear it, but you'll see that everyone has their own style.

The Cuadrilla : guys who meet in preschool and keep meeting through the rest of their lives. You often see groups of four, or five, or six or more in the town.

NOVEMBER - AZAROA

This boat has been in dry dock having work done for at least the 18 months we have lived in Hondarribia.

As it is at all times of year, the weather is variable, but November is very much so. In our first year, we were sitting outside having menu del dias a lot of the time (one weekend it hit 28°C). I was paddling across to France at least once a week to surf. In the second year, it was cold and wet and the River Bidasoa flushed mud, branches and unmentionables out into Txingudi Bay, making it very uninviting.

RUBBISH

One of the reasons there are so many branches and leaves in the estuary at this time of year is the council's method of green waste disposal. Perhaps it is because of the sheer volume of green waste they have. Before the town's plane trees lose all their leaves, they are pollarded. Most of the branches are cut off, leaving the bulbous stumps. Since Calle San Pedro is an avenue of dozens of plane trees and they are dotted around many more of Hondarribia's streets, there are a lot of branches to dispose of. Their ingenious solution to this is to collect them up, dump them on the ramp by the estuary at low tide, saw any large trunks into smaller pieces and leave the tide to remove them. The estuary is full of logs, branches and leaves for weeks after and it makes crossing the river on a body board rather more hazardous than normal. It's also a terrible waste of organic material that could be used as mulch, or rotted down to great compost.

The dumping of the town's prunings is part of the schizophrenic attitude to waste disposal. Though the town throws tree branches and leaves in the river, it collects household organic waste for composting. Similarly, the council provides masses of litter bins, which are dotted around the town, but a large minority of people ignore them and throw their rubbish on the ground. This ingrained behaviour is most evident in bars, where people will deliberately toss their paper napkins on the floor, or even in the street. Unfortunately, this is copied by the kids, who toss their less biodegradable crisp and sweet wrappers in the street too.

Households don't have their own bins to be collected by the council. Instead, there are community bins in every block. They are organised into general rubbish, glass, containers (plastic and metal) and paper, and they are emptied daily. Many neighbours ignore this organisation and dump their rubbish into the nearest bin available. You will also see larger items dumped next to the bins for collection. Amazingly, they get picked up eventually. The most distressing thing is that you often see new things in the bins, even unused and in their original packaging. There isn't much of a culture of second hand or charity shops in Spain (the notable exception in this area is Emaus, a charity that runs out of Irun and has shops there and in Donostia-San Sebastian). When people get tired of their stuff, or move, they often just throw it out and buy something new.

PLANE TREES

As the plane trees lose their leaves, they look more sculptural. The avenue of Calle San Pedro is formed of severely pollarded trees with very bulbous branches. In the carpark near Alameda restaurant and up at the Cantina de Guadalupe, the young branches have been pleached so that they have grown to form a lattice of interlinking limbs overhead.

Most of the tourists are long gone by November and the town bars are full of locals. Like the rest of Spain, Basque people tend to socialise by going out. You are rarely invited to people's houses for drinks, or dinner. When we did have friends around for a couple of housewarming drinks, they ended up staying for hours, so perhaps it is just safer to meet in the street. It can be difficult to buy people a round of drinks too, but we discovered that if you say that it is your invitation ("Te invito"), that is usually enough to silence any protest!

INTERCAMBIO

We met many of our friends through Spanish-English exchanges: Intercambio. If you are in the Basque Country to learn Spanish, it's an ideal way to improve your conversational Spanish. Initially, we put up signs to see if any locals would be interested. Then we were contacted by an American, Terra, who said there was already a group in Hondarribia. So we joined that. At the time of writing, we were meeting every Thursday (pincho-pote night, where you can get a drink and a pincho for 2 euros in many bars) at 6.30 in Hotel Obispo to speak for an hour in Castilian Spanish and an hour in English. A great way to learn and a great group of people.

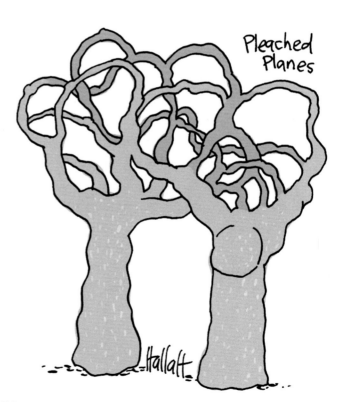

Pleached Planes

DECEMBER – ABENDUA

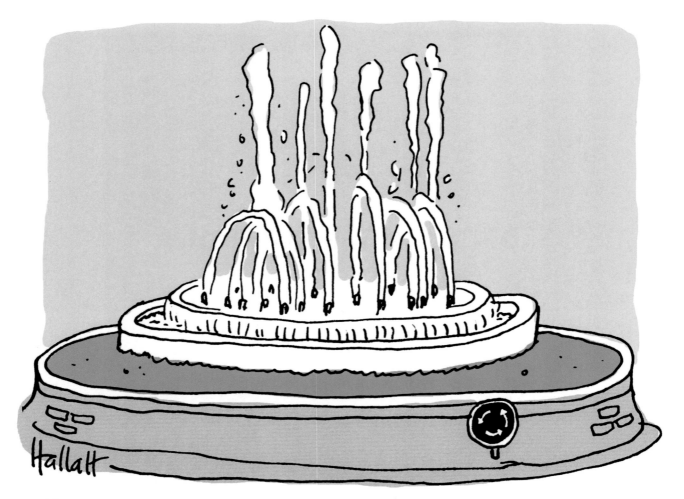

Hondarribia has a fountain in the middle of a roundabout. It seems to be on at random, or maybe it is on when drivers obey the road rules of a roundabout (infrequently).

Our first December in Hondarribia was freakishly warm. I was surfing right up until New Year. On Christmas Day we walked one of the tracks on Jaizkibel and had a picnic lunch in short sleeves. The second December was also quite mild, though not as settled.

PUENTES

The 6th December is Constitution Day and on the 8th it is the Day of the Immaculate Conception. Both are Spanish holidays. The Basques may not care for observing Spanish customs, but they do like a holiday. When there are two of them, or they occur near a weekend, the Spanish call them a "puente". This means "bridge" as they often take off the intervening days and connect the holidays together to make a bigger one. The second year we were there, the 6th and the 8th were on a Tuesday and Thursday, so many people took the whole week off. It was a period of calm, sunny, 15 degree days and felt like spring, as we walked down Calle San Pedro. The tables were busting with people making the most of the holiday and the weather.

SANTO TOMAS

The festival on 21st December doesn't seem to be a holiday, as the banks and many shops remain open. Both Hondarribia and Donostia-San Sebastian host extensive markets of local produce and artisan goods. Though Donostia's is bigger and busier, we found Hondarribia's market to be just as good. Traditionally, Santo Tomás was a day when tenant farmers would come into town to pay their landlords. Though a lot of the locals dress up in their traditional costumes, they aren't here to pay any dues. They are here to eat a LOT of txistorra (chistorra). Some of it is sold with a talo, or homemade corn (maize) pancake, and it is like eating the best hot dog you ever had. You need to queue for the superior stuff, so look for the line when you are walking around the txistorra stalls.

BASQUE CHRISTMAS & NEW YEAR

It is easy to be caught unawares by Christmas and miss the last posting dates for packages to be sent abroad. The shops don't go crazy with Christmas decorations and the lights don't go up in the streets until the end of November, being switched on on 1st December. You aren't bombarded with piped Christmas music and you aren't surrounded with reminders to BUY BUY BUY. There are few chain stores in the town and the cafés and restaurants carry on their business as usual.

That is until Olentzero starts to show up. Effigies of a slightly pudgy man, usually asleep, always with a pouch of wine, Basque clothing and a large beret (txapela/boina), appear in shop windows. Some of the older legends about Olentzero describe him as a scary charcoal maker who came out of the woods and terrorised children if they didn't behave. We like that idea. The modern Olentzero is basically a rival to the overly-commercial, Americanised Father Christmas and the Spanish Three Kings. Like them, he gives presents to children, but he does it on Christmas Eve. In the run up to Christmas, a substantial shed appears in Hondarribia's Gipuzkoa Square, complete with a bed, household utensils and everything that a drunken, middle-aged man needs to minister to children. In the week before Christmas, children line up to post their requests to Olentzero through his letterbox. The day before Christmas Eve, guys dressed in sheepskins with bells on their bottoms parade around (we found out from our Intercambio friends that they are Joaldunak. See February, for more.). Then on Christmas Eve evening, an effigy of Olentzero shows up in the square so that children can tell him their wishes. Weirdly, on Christmas Day, it seems like nothing happens at all and people are out in Calle San Pedro, eating and drinking as normal.

New Year's Eve is a big night, as in the UK, with a lot of drinking and setting off of fireworks. There is a Spanish tradition of eating a grape on each chime of midnight, to bring good luck. We went up to Arma Plaza to do this to the bells of the paroquia... and they didn't ring! It seemed strange that the chimes are considerate of local residents, as normally the Spanish aren't too concerned about making a racket at night. It was a bit of a let-down using our phones to see in the New Year instead. There were no organised celebrations, but we wandered the

Olentzero

streets of the old town and found every man and his dog letting off fireworks, all over the place. The bridge out of the north gate was a good spot to watch the haphazard displays before heading home.

OUR FAVOURITE HONDARRIBIA BARS, CAFES AND RESTAURANTS

There are tons of good bars and restaurants in Hondarribia and it is great to wander around and follow the crowds to see what is popular at the moment. There were some places that we kept going back to and these are our personal choices.

OLD TOWN

Hotel Palacete, Gipuzkoa Square

Unlike the place we call "Green Tables" (recently changed to white ones), across the square, Hotel Palacete looks expensive, but is very reasonable. It is a great place to sit outside in the summer with a glass of wine and is popular with locals for coffee.

Antxiña, Arma Plaza

You can go to the Parador and have a drink at the bar if you don't mind paying the inflated prices for a view of the inside of Carlos V's castle. It is worth it for one drink, at least, but a few steps away is the dog-friendly and better priced Antxiña. It is a classic, long, skinny bar that usually has good pinchos, and good food when the kitchen is open. The wine and cider are cheap and you can try and butter up the bartender to get a good pour of beer... Good luck - we don't call this place "Grumpy Guy's" for no reason. The rest of the staff are super nice!

Hotel Obispo, Obispo Square

There's a square on the east side of the old town that is the place to hang out on a sunny afternoon. This is Obispo (Bishop) square and it's below the paroquia (the large church with the clock tower). The hotel on the southern side makes good pinchos and is the only place we know of that has an open fire in the winter. If you walk through past this lounge room, and out the back, there is a sweet little terrace. In the second year we were there, they opened a gastro bar, but after an initial flurry the crowds returned to Etxeberria next door.

Etxeberria, Obispo Square

This bar has tables on Obispo square and runs through to Calle Mayor on the other side. It does some of the best bar pinchos and the bocadillos (big sandwiches) are good value. Their range of wines is good and, if you are missing decent beer (ales), this is the place to go, though you'll pay a lot more than for the average Spanish caña.

Hotel Palacete looks posh, but, unlike the grungy "Green Tables" opposite, it is a very affordable place to have a drink.

Danonzat, Denda Kalea

Gorka runs this cute little wine bar on one of the roads that leads off the Calle Mayor. He is a great host and salesman and often appears in the local press with his pincho creations. However, we rarely see the same pinchos on the bar. It's worth showing up on a Thursday out of season to try his pincho pote, when you will get a good deal for a couple of euros. At the time of writing, he had just installed a pizza oven to make thin crust pizzas.

JUST OUTSIDE THE OLD TOWN, BELOW THE SOUTH GATE

Bar Larra

Most locals prefer Batzokia, across the square, but Bar Larra is one of our favourite places for a menu del dia (11 euros midweek and 18-20 at the weekend, so go midweek - it's the same food). It is great to sit out in the square and people watch, but in the cooler months (or rain), there is a covered area that you can still bring your dog into.

Alameda: Minasoroeta Kalea, 1

This is the only restaurant in Hondarribia with a Michelin star and if you like that kind of fancy, over-thought food, it could be the place for you. We enjoyed our dinner there, but the enormous room lacks ambience and caters better to the many weddings that it hosts. Far more fun is the little bar that faces the road. There is no outside seating, but you can take dogs inside (it is small, so large dogs might not be so welcome) and the bar menu has really interesting pinchos and raciones. There is a good wine list that lets you try a lot of decent drops by the glass.

MARINA (IN CALLE SAN PEDRO, UNLESS NOTED)

Amona Margarita

We had no internet in our first flat and Amona (meaning "grandmother" in Basque) was a godsend, as the wifi is free and fast. The coffee is the best in town, though that isn't saying much, as coffee is pretty average in most of Spain (the one place we found that did anything close to Melbourne standards was Sakona in Donostia-San Sebastian.). Amona is also a bakery and makes great sourdough bread and some pretty fine napolitanas (pain au chocolate).

Txantxangorri

This unassuming little bar decked out in white and green is very popular with locals. Its menu has the usual suspects, but the execution is a touch above the norm. We became addicted to the txipirones a la plancha (grilled baby squid).

Bar Ondarribi

A little way down from Txantxangorri is Bar Ondarribi, which has been renovated recently to make it a little more swish. You can get the local Bidasoa Brewing Company beer on tap. It is worth standing at the bar for a drink and seeing what imaginative pinchos emerge from the kitchen so that you can eat them while they are still fresh. The jamón with quail's egg, is great.

Conchita

Super-friendly staff, dogs are allowed in and they nearly always have excellent pulpo pinchos on the bar.

My weakness —
"Napolitanas",
or pain au
chocolate

Hallatt

Robin   Txantxangorri

I only know this ↑ Basque
word because it is the
name of a great restaurant
in Hondarribia. Hallalt

Bar Zabala

Out of season, many bars offer a drink (usually wine, or a small beer) and a pincho on a Thursday night for a couple of euros. Zabala is the only place that does "pincho pote" all the time. Some of the pinchos are clearly mass-produced and cooked from frozen, but the tortilla is good, as are the homemade quiche and Gildas.

Gran Sol

One of the pricier bars, but good quality and with a huge (in summer, enormous) array of pinchos on the bar. They are all priced the same, so some are better value than others. If you can get the little oblong tarts when they are still warm from the kitchen, they are to die for.

Ardoka

A great little wine bar, that is dog and boyfriend-friendly. There is an amazing range of wine by the glass and you don't have to stand outside in bad weather. It is the perfect place to try the different grape varieties that Spain has to offer (like most bars, you are unlikely to find much wine from further afield, but who cares when the local stuff is so good?). They have a few good pinchos on the bar, but you get the best ones if you order their hot pinchos from the kitchen. They are better value for money and more interesting than in most bars.

Senra

This doesn't have the same ambience as Ardoka next door and it doesn't allow dogs inside, but Senra has fantastic pinchos, a good range of wine and Amba beer on tap.

Itsaspe

Right at the end of the street is a pretty bar/restaurant that is popular with the locals and dog-friendly. The drinks are slightly more expensive and the menu is a little pricey, but the pinchos on the bar are good value. The best place to be in the summer is at one of the outside tables, if you can find one.

Leize: Santiago Kalea, 65

If you want to go to a very Basque bar, this is your place. It is run by a young guy who speaks English and Spanish, but will try and teach you Basque if he sees you often enough. The pinchos are basic, but fairly priced and you get a good pour of beer. It is very popular with the cuadrillas of younger men.

THE BEACH

Just back from the town beach are a stretch of bars that face on to the marina. The outside tables are great for drinking a cold beer and watching the world go by. There is a burger place up top that does the best burger we have had in Hondarribia, but I should point out that burgers aren't really a Spanish speciality. A much better place to go for lunch is Curry Verde, a vegetarian restaurant that will even please non-veggies with its interesting food. The wines are organic and bottles you are unlikely to see in other restaurants.

WALKING DISTANCE

A 20 minute walk out of town takes you to Laia, which is a cut above the normal restaurant in quality and only slightly more in price (menu del dia is 24 euros, but worth it).

If you want a better walk and cheap, homestyle cooking, ask the tourist information centre for directions to the Cantina de Guadalupe. You can walk up past caseríos and a bar (Errandonea), through a bamboo forest and via stations of the cross to reach the cantina. It is a jumping off point for all kinds of walks in the hills.

OTHER BASQUE PLACES
WE LOVED

I wish I could withstand the cold water to surf at Zurriola in the winter like these guys.
Hallatt

This list is personal, rather than exhaustive, but these are the places we liked enough to go back to, time and time again:

DONOSTIA-SAN SEBASTIAN
A short bus ride away and very touristy if you stick to the old town, but there is a lot more to explore in Donostia. Climbing the hill to Jesus (Monte Urgull) is a must, to see the views of Gros and Zurriola surf beach on one side and the calm bay of La Concha on the other.

If you walk, or take the bus to the other side of La Concha, you can see the fantastic iron sculptures by the esteemed Basque artist, Eduardo Chillida. You can carry on walking up to Monte Igueldo, or take the funicular. At the top, you'll find a century-old amusement park, which is worth going to for the rickety rollercoaster ride alone. You can even ride it with a dog, but we don't recommend it, as Billie was nearly as scared as my 4 year old nephew (also not recommended for under 5's).

Gros is getting to be the hip side of town, with excellent coffee at Sakona and a few cool cafés, bars and pincho places dotted around the streets behind the beach. It's a pleasant walk along the river to the new cultural complex of Tabakalera (the old tobacco factory), where there is another bar and free exhibitions.

TOLOSA
Tolosa used to be the capital of Gipuzkoa (now it's Donostia) and it's still a vibrant town. It sits across the banks of the Oria river and is a great place to wander around, taking in the narrow streets of the old town, with their variety of independent shops and pincho bars. The Saturday market is one of the best in the area and there is a café directly opposite (Solana.4) that does great coffee.

We rarely buy bottled water, as the tap water is fine to drink! But we sometimes buy stuff that comes in these bottles, like vermouth. They were selling a lot of milk in them at Tolosa market. Duncan **loves** fresh cow's milk, so he bought some.

It's sheep's milk.

Hallatt

PAMPLONA

We haven't been to Pamplona during San Fermin and the running of the bulls and neither do we want to. Watching animals being teased and later killed for entertainment isn't our thing. Neither is getting wasted with huge numbers of tourists. Outside of this time, Pamplona is our kind of place. It has lots of great bars and restaurants, growing environmental awareness, beautiful old town architecture and a large expanse of parks and green spaces.

ORDIZIA

Following the Oria further into the interior of Gipuzkoa you find Ordizia. There is a renowned market in this little town on a Wednesday morning. The central square is covered and you'll find an amazing variety of locally grown produce, cheese and preserved meats. We've rarely found fresh meat in Basque markets. Perhaps there is a law against it. The first time we went, the Dia del Pastor (Day of the Shepherd) fair was on and there were even more stalls, a lot of sheep and a massive barbecue. Fairs happen in Easter week, September and around Christmas and if your Spanish is any good, you can read more here: www.ordiziakoazoka.com.

GETARIA

This is still a cute little fishing village, but it can get overwhelmed by people on high days and holidays because of its small size and beautiful location. There are two sweet beaches. One is a sheltered swimming bay and the other usually has a decent, though small, break for surfers. If the water isn't too inviting, you can walk up the hill, San Antón (sometimes called El Ratón, "the mouse", which it looks like in profile), which has great views of the village and the surrounding txakoli vineyards and coastline.

Once you have worked up an appetite, there are plenty of pincho bars and a few places that do a decent menu del dia, though it is hard to find anything less than 20 euros given the prime waterfront location. You might want to check out the fashion museum in Getaria, the

Cristobal Balenciaga Museum, if you are into that kind of thing. If you are not, it's a lot more fun to walk along the coast path to Zarautz, which is surf central on this part of the coast.

BILBAO

You can drive to Bilbao in just over an hour from Hondarribia, if you don't have a 1975 Land Rover. We prefer to take the train from Donostia. It trundles along, stopping at every little town along the way, but the scenery is interesting and our dog was allowed on there on a lead.

Accommodation is inexpensive and the old town has a great collection of pincho bars and restaurants. It's fun to walk along the river up to the Guggenheim and marvel at the crazy architecture, but the outside is more impressive than the art within. A cheaper alternative is the Bella Artes museum nearby, which has a fantastic collection of Basque art.

MUTRIKU

To be honest, we only went here twice and that was because of the mackerel festival (see April). However, it is well worth it. The old town is well-preserved and has an amazing number of bars, considering its size. The port has been developed so that there are two swimming tidal pools, a small beach and a giant breakwater that is actually a wave energy plant. It has been feeding power to the grid since 2011.

You can walk from Mutriku, through the Flysch Geoparque (http://geoparkea.com), which is a stunning part of the Basque coast.

For more about where to go and what to do in these places, check out Duncan's Local Food Hound Blog: https://localfoodhound.wordpress.com.

FURTHER READING

Most of the information in this book is from what we've learned living here and speaking with the locals. However, there are a couple of sources that have given us more insight into the Basque culture:

THE BASQUE HISTORY OF THE WORLD - MARK KURLANSKY

Though this book contains a lot of useful information and is a good primer on Basque history, I found it very disjointed and a bit of a slog to get through. And, as the Rough Guide to Spain points out, he is a bit of an apologist for ETA. Fortunately, the Basque Country has moved on a lot since this book was published in 2000.

THE RISE AND FALL OF ETA

https://thebluereview.org/rise-fall-eta/ A well-rounded description of how ETA came to be, how it warped into something horrific and its ultimate demise.

BUBER'S BASQUE PAGE

http://buber.net/Basque/ A treasure trove of all things Basque.

OTHER LINKS:

Local Food Hound
https://localfoodhound.wordpress.com My partner, Duncan, publishes a blog about food and our travels around Spain and beyond.

The source of the world "carnival":
https://www.visualthesaurus.com/cm/wordroutes/celebrating-an-etymological-carnival/

Tourist Information on Irun, Hondarribia and Hendaye:
http://www.irunhondarribiahendaye.com

Tourist Information on the Basque Country:
https://turismo.euskadi.eus
http://www.basquecountry-tourism.com

THANK YOU FOR READING

I hope you enjoyed this book. As an independent author and illustrator it would really help me if you left a review for it on Amazon, or Goodreads. A single line is fine!

If you'd like to receive illustrated emails about other things I'm working on, please subscribe to my mailing list: http://eepurl.com/cCOOeD

ABOUT THE AUTHOR

Alex Hallatt was born and brought up in the West Country in England. She emigrated to New Zealand, where she met her partner, Duncan and his dog, Billie. They spent a few years living in Australia, England and Spain and are now back in New Zealand.

You can see more of Alex's work at alexhallatt.com.

ALSO BY ALEX HALLATT

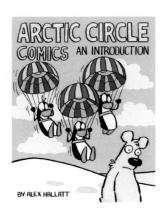

Arctic Circle Comics: An Introduction
Arctic Circle is about three penguins who have moved north. This cartoon collection introduces Oscar, Ed, Gordo and the other characters in this syndicated comic strip with an environmental theme.

50 Habits of Highly Effective Grey Tabby Cats
Why are cats the most popular pets in the country? This book of cat cartoons explains all. Well, maybe not all, but certainly 50 reasons cats are very effective pets.

FAB (Friends Against Bullying) Club

For 8-12 year olds

If you were being bullied, what would you do? What if you could join a club that could make the bullying stop? This is the story of how the best ever club got started.

Friends Against Bullying - Join the Club!

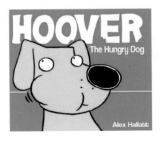

Hoover the Hungry Dog

For preschoolers

Hoover is always hungry and often eats things he shouldn't, with hilarious consequences.

Made in the USA
San Bernardino, CA
24 June 2019